To our beautiful children—Iyannah, Nala, Jerimiah, Ameyah, Josiah, and to our ever-curious spark, Aveyah—thank you. Each of you is the rhythm of our hearts and the reason this story lives on these pages. It was Aveyah's tender questions, filled with wonder, that first lit the flame of this book. Through her voice, God whispered a reminder: every child deserves to see the beauty of the family He has so carefully woven together. A very special thank you to Anita Clinton and Nia Obotette, who stepped into this vision with us in 2021. Your time, your wisdom, and your care gave breath to what was only an idea. You helped water the seed God planted, and we are forever grateful. And to you, dear reader, holding this book now—you are part of this story too. May these pages remind you that family is not bound by blood alone but by the divine thread of love that God Himself knits around us. Whether blended, extended, or born in unexpected ways, family is His masterpiece. "God places the lonely in families; He sets the prisoners free and gives them joy." —Psalm 68:6 Our prayer is that as you turn each page, you see reflections of your own family's beauty and God's hand at work within it. May He bless your home with unity, fill your hearts with peace, and strengthen every bond with a love that never fails. No matter how He has brought you together—you are family, and you are His.

Up on the hill in the Sunshine House, in the town of Merrysville, lived the Wallaces. There was Alex, the dad; Eryn, his wife; and their two children, Calvin and Georgia.

Georgia was a child who viewed life through a different lens. She saw the world as a place where she could use her imagination to create. She was always filled with hope and knew she had many opportunities before her to create new things. The excitement beamed on her face as she took to the lawn to play one golden Friday afternoon.

As she was in the middle of making her incredibly special sun-baked dandelion cream mud pie, Georgia was on her way to pick out the most beautiful flowers to top off her featured dessert. Her search was interrupted as something caught her attention. Floating up their driveway was an unidentified silver object that transported an unknown gentleman right to their front door.

As the doorbell rang, Georgia quietly
crept closer, leaving her toys behind, so
she could listen to voices as they
started to talk:

"Hello, I am here to pick up Calvin," said
the unknown man.

"Sure thing," Georgia's dad Alex said.
"Come on in."

As Georgia moved in closer, she could see her brother gathering his favorite suitcase and heading out the front door with the visitor.

Georgia felt green with envy. She wanted to join Calvin. How could he leave without her? Where was he going and who was he going with? Her slow, subtle movements suddenly turned into rushed steps as she came down the stairway and onto the first floor.

"Daddy," Georgia said, "who was that and why did he only come to get Calvin?"

"Don't be blue," Alex said. "Let us take a walk together. I want to show you something."

Georgia's mom, Eryn, grabbed their coats and kissed them both. "Be back before dinner!" she called out after them.

"Will do!" said Alex.

As they walked down the road and headed toward the first corner, Georgia asked, "So where is my brother and who was he with?" as if her father hadn't heard her the first time.

"I want to show you something; do you mind taking a walk with me?" said Alex.

"Sure, Daddy!" exclaimed Georgia, "but where are we going?"

"Just around the neighborhood," he said.

As they started their journey, they came upon a house that stood out from the other houses around it due to its magnificent mandarin- orange color.

"Do you ever notice the orange house on the corner, the one with the shutters?"
"Why yes, Daddy!" she said. "That is where my friend Oscar lives. We go to the same school. Is Calvin at Oscar's house?"
"No, but do you know why I brought you here?"
"No," Georgia answered quietly.

"This house represents joy. Before Oscar's siblings came along, Oscar found it very lonely as an only child. His parents could not have any more children on their own, but they were determined to continue growing their family, so they adopted his siblings," Alex explained.

"This brought joy into their home and to their family.

Their bond brings them strength and encouragement every day!"

As they continued to walk a little further,
they came to the red house in their
neighborhood.

"Why are we stopping here, Daddy?"
Georgia asked.

"This house belongs to the Garcia family.
Mrs. Garcia takes care of her nieces and
nephews so they can all grow up
together."

"They did not see much of their father and lost their mother in the war in Iraq. To keep them from being separated, Mrs. Garcia took them all in."

"They do not get a chance to go on visits like Calvin, but they are with family, and that has brought them so much love and good energy."

As they continued their walk they came to the pink house.

"This is my favorite house in the neighborhood, Daddy," said Georgia.

"And why is that, Georgia?" asked Alex.

"Because it makes me think of sweetness and kindness," she said.

"You are exactly right, sweetheart!"

"Mr. Anderson lives in the pink house," said Alex.

"I know Mr. Anderson," Georgia said. "I play with his daughters Chloe and Michelle all the time."

"Did you know that both Chloe and Michelle did not have the same mother, but they both live with their father?" Alex asked Georgia.

"Mr. Anderson was married to Chloe's mom, but she passed away soon after giving birth to her. Then he met Michelle's mom, but their relationship was not successful. Mr. Anderson vowed to continue to raise his girls together and show them that they are still a family. It has been a challenge to raise his daughters on his own, without the help of a mother, but Mr. Anderson has done so much for his girls by continuing to be the best father he can be!"

"He painted the house pink as a symbol of his love for his daughters," said Alex.

Georgia began to smile as the colors began to resonate within her.

As they turned the block to head home, they came across the white house right down the street from their home.

"Dad," said Georgia, "I know who lives here!"

"Who, Georgia?" Alex replied.

"This is the home of the Johnsons," she said excitedly.

"That's right, Georgia! Mrs. Johnson is raising her three grandchildren. She is bringing them so much goodness after the loss of their parents. The Johnson children grew up in a tough neighborhood and witnessed a lot of bad things. Their father and mother did not make good choices and they are incarcerated because of their decisions. Thanks to their grandmother, the Johnson kids have had opportunities to make better choices and achieve great things."

"Now they have a bright path thanks to their grandmother," said Alex.

"You see, Georgia, each family is different, but together they build a beautiful spectrum of colors that shine a light of love into each family."

"What about our house, Daddy?" asked

Georgia.

"Why do we have a yellow house?"

"Our house is named the Sunshine House because of its beautiful yellow color. Your mom said she loved the color yellow because of the way it made her feel. She said she loved yellow because it could bring happiness—whether you wore it, grew it, or even lived inside it."

"We experience happiness every day in our beautiful yellow house."

Our happiness comes from the love we share within our family.

"Yellow is also the color your mom said she felt the day we were married," Alex explained to Georgia.

"Before you, your mom had your brother Calvin. Although I am not Calvin's biological father, I love him just the same, and that brings joy to your mom."

"Once we were a family, we welcomed you into our lives and our happiness grew!"

"Today we work with Calvin's family to make sure he has a strong bond with them too."

"Just like Oscar's family?" Georgia asked.

"Yes, Georgia," said Alex.

"And Mrs. Garcia?" she asked as the excitement grew.

"That's right," said Alex.

"And Mr. Anderson?" she said as she looked as if she was going to burst.

"Yep!" said Alex.

"And Mrs. Johnson?" She said

"Of Course," Replied Dad

"And us!" she stated as she jumped with

joy.

"You got it, honey!" said Alex.

As the weekend came to a close, Mr. Richardson's silver truck returned and brought Calvin right to the front door. This time Georgia was waiting at the front door. She opened it even before Calvin's father could ring the doorbell.

"You're family!" exclaimed Georgia.

"Why, yes I am, Georgia," stated Mr. Richardson. "It's so nice to meet you. I've heard so much about you."

Georgia welcomed her brother back home, and they gathered upstairs in the playroom, excited to catch up with each other.

As Calvin gave Georgia all the details of his trip and his family visit, Georgia told her brother of the beauty she discovered in the colors all around them.

Georgia stood proudly in the picture window of her family's home, the Sunshine House. She looked out over the hill at her neighborhood and saw a rainbow of love in her community.

She thought to herself: even though each family was different and worked in many ways, each family together formed the most beautiful rainbow of love for all to see.